T0036949

THE ABSINTHE FRAPPÉ

MARIELLE SONGY

LOUISIANA STATE UNIVERSITY PRESS
BATON ROUGE

Published by Louisiana State University Press
lsupress.org

Manufactured in the United States of America
First printing

Designer: Barbara Neely Bourgoyne
Typeface: Arno Pro
Printer and binder: Integrated Books International (IBI)

Cover and frontispiece images: Absinthe frappé, courtesy photographer
Sam Gregory Anselmo.

Library of Congress Cataloging-in-Publication Data
Names: Songy, Marielle, author.
Title: The absinthe frappé / Marielle Songy.
Description: Baton Rouge : Louisiana State University Press, [2023] |
Includes bibliographical references.
Identifiers: LCCN 2022031002 | ISBN 978-0-8071-7929-1 (cloth)
Subjects: LCSH: Absinthe—History. | Cocktails. | Absinthe in art. | LCGFT:
  Cookbooks.
Classification: LCC TP607.A3 S66 2023 | DDC 641.2/5509—dc23/eng/20220725
LC record available at https://lccn.loc.gov/2022031002

*This book is dedicated to my father and my fiancé and
was written in memory of my late mother.*

CONTENTS

ACKNOWLEDGMENTS

When I began researching the absinthe frappé, I fell in love with the story and rich history of absinthe. There are so many layers to the absinthe story; putting all of the pieces in order was a process. It took a village, and *The Absinthe Frappé* wouldn't have happened without the help of many.

First and foremost, I want to thank Jenny Keegan, Alisa Plant, and the entire staff of LSU Press not only for approaching me with this project but for trusting me with it. This process has been a fantastic adventure, and throughout the writing of this book, Jenny helped me every step of the way. She was patient and kind with every question I had, and *The Absinthe Frappé* wouldn't exist without her. Women like Jenny are making a difference in the literary world, and I'm happy to be on her team.

I was already familiar with absinthe when I embarked on this journey, but I admit that I knew little of its origin or that of the absinthe frappé. So, when beginning my research, I started with the book, *Absinthe: History in a Bottle,* by Barnaby Conrad III. Absinthe lovers in my life told me that this is the "bible" of absinthe information, and I devoured it. I was immediately drawn to the history and mystery of absinthe and how it has touched so many facets of things we love, such as the art of Vincent van Gogh and the writing of Oscar Wilde.

From there, I moved on to Phil Baker's *The Book of Absinthe,* which filled out more of the story of this mesmerizing liquor. These two books provided the base of *The Absinthe Frappé* and made me want to delve deeper and learn more about the people involved in its history.

I knew that I wanted to tell the story of absinthe and the absinthe frappé in the most accurate way possible. However, researching something that has a history dating back over two hundred years is tricky. Records aren't always available, and I came upon some conflicting details in my exploration—many times I was forced to "split the difference" between sources of information. Thankfully, I had some experts on hand to guide me through parts of the process.

I sought out Ray Bordelon, an absinthe historian who has been studying all things absinthe for over twenty years. He answered my questions, filled in the blanks, and helped me get all of my dates straight. If you want to know about absinthe, Ray is the one with whom you have to speak. He knows *everything* about absinthe, and he was an invaluable source in this project. The question "Have you talked to Ray?" became a regular inquiry throughout my research. This book would not have been complete without his knowledge and expertise.

Elizabeth M. Williams, author and historian, founded the Southern Food & Beverage Museum in New Orleans. Inside this beautiful museum, which is a tribute to all things food and drink, is La Galerie de l'Absinthe, an absinthe museum that Elizabeth and Ray Bordelon have curated. You can find everything here from antique absinthe bottles and spoons to newspaper clippings and a replica absinthe fountain that Bordelon built himself. I was pinching myself when I realized the most spectacular absinthe museum in the United States is right here in my own backyard. If you are a local, visit the Southern Food & Beverage Museum tomorrow. If you're not a local, put the Southern Food & Beverage Museum on your list of New Orleans places to visit. Elizabeth and La Galerie de l'Absinthe added more pieces to the puzzle and gave my book depth.

I was so fortunate that I was able to speak with Theodore Breaux, an absinthe expert and distiller who had a hand in getting the restrictions on absinthe lifted in the United States. I was able to hear firsthand the story of the process, and like so many others who helped me with this book, he added another layer to the absinthe story. He was always available to answer any questions I had, no matter how obscure. I enjoyed learning about how Theodore makes and sells authentic absinthe through his company Jade Liqueurs and his creation of Lucid Absinthe Supérieure. If you ever want to talk absinthe or have any pressing questions, seek out Theodore and have a conversation—you will definitely learn something.

Jedd Haas at Atelier Vie Distillery in New Orleans was so welcoming and happy to explain the process of absinthe distilling and the history of his distillery, and he let me sample some of his absinthe. I still think that Toulouse Green is some of the smoothest absinthe that I've had the opportunity to try, and I thank Jedd for explaining his distillation process.

David Rodrigue took beautiful photos for *The Absinthe Frappé,* and this book wouldn't have been what it is without his work. Dave is a longtime friend who typically photographs historic antiques at M. S. Rau, landscapes, and figure models. I appreciate him taking the time to hop around to different bars with me and snap various versions of the frappé.

Finally, I want to thank the myriad bartenders and bars that let me sample different versions of the absinthe frappé and answer my questions about their preparation. I especially want to thank Bar Tonique, the Columns hotel, Cure, Hermes Bar, Mr. B's Bistro, the Old Absinthe House, and Pirate's Alley Café.

THE
ABSINTHE
FRAPPÉ

INTRODUCTION

Absinthe is a conversation starter. Made from wormwood, anise, and fennel and long associated with rumor and legend, it's a drink often misinterpreted as something dangerous or destructive—something that one should avoid.

In the mid-nineteenth century, absinthe took parts of Europe, especially France, by storm. The drink's allure continued into the early twentieth century, until it was unjustly banned due to the false belief that it led those who consumed it to madness.

The city most closely associated with absinthe in the United States is New Orleans. Much of the nineteenth-century population here held loyalty to France, with many retaining the country's language and customs.

The absinthe frappé was invented in New Orleans by Cayetano Ferrér at the Old Absinthe House. More than just a bartender, Ferrér was once an owner of the Old Absinthe House, and he and his family are credited with putting the bar, and the absinthe frappé served there, on the map. This cool mix of absinthe, simple syrup, and soda water, served over crushed ice, was so popular that in 1905 a song was written in its honor. At the time, the frappé was served in other cities throughout the United States, but here in New Orleans is where it was most popular until absinthe was banned in 1912.

Although there were absinthe substitutes on the market, the allure of the frappé fell out of fashion, and the cocktail has been primarily forgotten save for a few cocktail lovers and exclusive bars that continue to serve it. Of course, the cocktail is still available at the Old Absinthe House and other fine cocktail bars throughout New Orleans—you just have to know where to look.

While researching this book, I visited several New Orleans cocktail bars and found the frappé served in many different ways. Cure and Pirate's Alley Café make theirs traditionally, with absinthe, simple syrup, and soda water over crushed ice. At Bar Tonique, they forgo the ice and serve the drink straight up. At Hermes Bar, rather than use simple syrup, they light a sugar cube on fire and mix the melted sugar into the absinthe and soda water; it is then served over crushed ice. At Mr. B's Bistro, they make their frappé neat in a martini glass with an added egg white—another classic variation of the cocktail. Finally, at Old Absinthe House, you can order a traditional absinthe frappé or opt for an "Herbsaint frappé" made with an absinthe substitute.

To fully appreciate the absinthe frappé, you must first know the history of absinthe—the frappé's star ingredient. First distilled in 1792, absinthe is rich in history and played a role in many realms, from art to science. To the best of my knowledge, no other liquor influenced so many different aspects of nineteenth-century society and life as absinthe.

I hope that by the end of this book, you'll not only have learned something but you'll be motivated to try an absinthe frappé for yourself (or even make one!). A glass of absinthe is a glass of history, mystery, and magic.

CHAPTER ONE

THE MYSTERIOUS ELIXIR

A HISTORY OF ABSINTHE

To fully appreciate the absinthe frappé, you have to know the history of absinthe, the liquor that is the heart and soul of the cocktail. Absinthe didn't start as a social liquor that brought people together and inspired nineteenth-century artists. Instead, it was first used as a medicinal tonic.

It's hard to pinpoint precisely when absinthe was first consumed. Wormwood, an herb that is a significant ingredient in absinthe, dates back to ancient Egypt; the ancient Greeks used wormwood extracts as a medicinal remedy. Their word for the bitter herb was *apsinthion,* meaning "undrinkable." It is believed that, during this time, Hippocrates made a wormwood-flavored wine that was said to cure digestive disorders and ease anemia and rheumatism. It was also thought to prevent lice and act as an antidote to poisonous reptile and bug bites.

The Ebers Papyrus, an anthology of Egyptian medical texts of herbal knowledge dating to 1550 BCE, describes wormwood as a medicinal herb. It suggests that the plant was used as a tonic, an antiseptic, and a remedy for fever and other minor ailments. There was also a belief that wormwood could prevent drunkenness and cure syphilis. While there is no proof that it was effective, it is clear that wormwood was long considered a "cure-all."

In the seventeenth century, Madame de Coulanges, a leading lady of the French court, was prescribed a wormwood elixir to calm her stomach. She was so taken with its medicinal effects that she considered it a cure for all that ailed her. "My little absinthe is the remedy for all diseases," she wrote to her cousin Madame de Sévigné. Around the same time, it was thought that wormwood could be a protection against the plague. People would sleep with it under their pillows and burn it in their homes to "purify" plague-infected air.

Before the absinthe with which we are familiar, people consumed wormwood in other drinks. Absinthites oinos was a wormwood-flavored wine made by steeping the leaves of the wormwood plant in wine; it was drunk by the ancient Greeks. In 1559 London apothecaries were no longer the only place where you could get distilled medicinal wine, so independent distilleries began making their own potent potables. One such drink was a wormwood ale known as purl. It was created by infusing warm ale with the tops of various species of wormwood, most notably *Artemisia maritima*, which grows in coastal salt marshes. These drinks eventually fell out of fashion, and the consumption of wormwood was largely forgotten.

MODERN ABSINTHE TAKES SHAPE

As the story goes, absinthe, in the sense of the distilled spirit, was invented in 1792 by the retired French physician Dr. Pierre Ordinaire. Ordinaire was fleeing the French Revolution when he settled in the Swiss village of Couvet. There he found *Artemisia absinthium,* or grande wormwood, growing wild in the Val-de-Travers region. He mixed the flowers and leaves of the plant with green anise, sweet fennel, and other medicinal herbs. The fennel and anise gave absinthe its licorice-like taste, while wormwood added bitterness to the mix and gave absinthe its green hue. The combination of green anise, sweet fennel, and grande wormwood is considered "the Holy Trinity of Absinthe." Ordinaire's concoction was a 136-proof elixir that became a panacea called "La Fée verte," or the Green Fairy.

According to legend, while on his deathbed, Ordinaire passed the recipe for absinthe to two sisters by the name of Henriod. However, the story of Ordinaire having invented absinthe is widely questioned. The more likely truth is that the ladies were the actual inventors of the drink, having sold it in Switzerland since the 1760s. Thus, it's probable that Dr. Ordinaire simply promoted La Fée verte as an elixir.

It is believed that Frenchman Major Henri Dubied bought a bottle of absinthe from the Henriod sisters in

1797, after discovering that it was a fantastic remedy for indigestion, chills, fever, coughs, and lack of appetite. Major Dubied then began marketing absinthe with his son, Marcellin, and his son-in-law, Henri-Louis Perrenoud, in Couvet. From there, the three produced absinthe in their distillery and sold it to the masses. In 1805 Perrenoud split from Dubied. He changed his name to "Pernod," opened Pernod Fils distillery, and moved production from Switzerland to Pontarlier, France, to avoid import taxes.

Because this is two hundred–year–old history, it's easy for the facts to get lost in the shuffle. During my research, I came across the name Abram-Louis Perrenoud—the father of Henri-Louis. Some sources suggest that *he* was the first to distill absinthe in Couvet, so I reached out to absinthe expert Theodore Breaux to see if he could help make sense of this information.

Breaux explained: "Abram-Louis Perrenoud is regarded as the originator of the first commercial [absinthe] operation in Couvet, Switzerland, circa 1794. The nature of his association with Major Dubied at this time seems to be unclear. Dubied may have been a partner and financier, with Perrenoud in charge of the operations. Perrenoud's untimely death precipitated a chain of events that muddy the waters. It appears that he either sold or bequeathed his ownership and control to Major Dubied, leaving his son, Henri-Louis, as an employee (distiller) or lesser partner. As such, the history of the Pernod brand is focused upon 1805, which is the year Henri-Louis departed the original business, relocated across the border to Pontarlier, and changed his surname to Pernod."

THE FRENCH FALL IN LOVE WITH THE GREEN FAIRY

In *Absinthe: History in a Bottle,* Barnaby Conrad III explains that the infatuation with absinthe in Paris began after the French colonial wars in Algeria. From 1844 to 1847, French troops were given absinthe, usually mixed with wine or water, to ward off fever and kill bacteria in the drinking water. When the soldiers returned to Paris, they had developed a taste for anise and wanted more of it. The Pernods' distillery, now being run by Henri-Louis's son, Louis, was happy to oblige. After Louis died, in 1850, his sons, Louis-Alfred and Fritz Pernod, took over the Pernod Fils factory under the guidance of their mother, Emilie, and with the support of Swiss engineer Arthur Borel, who designed the factory's equipment.

Absinthe was good for the people of Pontarlier. In a town of 8,776 people, 500 of them worked for Pernod and other distilleries. At the height of the liquor's popularity, Pontarlier had twenty-one absinthe distilleries. In 1873 Louis-Alfred and Fritz introduced a profit-sharing plan that provided workers' retirement pay—a revolutionary concept for the time.

The Pernods also provided their workers with accident insurance and unemployment compensation. This guaranteed that workers would receive half-wages if they were unable to work due to illness. The Pernod factory itself was a good place to work, as there was plenty of light and ventilation, and it was clean. Furthermore, half of the 170 workers who ran the twenty-six stills and twenty-two coloring tanks were women. The Pernod Fils factory was so efficient that by 1896 daily production was up to 125,000 liters a day.

By 1860 absinthe began to take hold of French culture, and its popularity soared among the rich and working class alike. The rising consumption of absinthe during this time is credited to the improvement of working wages and the difference in price between absinthe and France's other alcoholic drink of choice, wine. At its conception, absinthe was a rather expensive drink. However, the cost began to drop as more distilleries began producing it.

Admittedly, there were different qualities of absinthe— some were considered more "high end" than other brands. The best-quality absinthe was traditionally distilled using white grape alcohol. According to this method, dried wormwood, fennel, anise, and sometimes other botanicals were soaked in alcohol for a prescribed period in a process called maceration. Heat was then applied to the mixture, which was distilled into a perfumed spirit. During distillation, any unwanted flavors, like bitterness, were removed. The desired essences from the plants recondensed with the distillate, following which other herbs like hyssop and lemon balm were added to the mix. The chlorophyll from the leaves of these added herbs gives absinthe its familiar green color.

Lesser-quality absinthe was typically made with industrial alcohol as a base. It was cheaply and poorly made and contained harmful chemicals such as copper sulfate. According to absinthe historian Ray Bordelon, the makers of this "rotgut" absinthe preyed upon people who couldn't afford the higher-quality beverage. The cheaper absinthe made people sick and led to stories that absinthe was a harmful liquor.

THE ALLURE OF ABSINTHE TAKES HOLD

It wasn't just men who were enjoying absinthe; women enjoyed it as early as 1880. Earlier in the nineteenth century, cafés were male haunts, but the introduction of absinthe saw women sitting side by side, drinking with them. Women of all classes drank absinthe and seemed to take to it rather easily. Liquor sellers even suggested that women and absinthe were a good mix, claiming that women who imbibed the drink took their absinthe neat in the glass and without sugar. Whether or not this is true is a matter of speculation, but it does make for an interesting anecdote.

Absinthe's popularity can also be credited to sheer luck. In the mid-nineteenth century, wine prices soared when French vineyards were infested with phylloxera, an insect that attacked grape plants' roots. The bug destroyed two-thirds of the wine fields of Europe, devastating the industry. Moreover, the "Great French Wine Blight," as it was called, made the wine that was available quite expensive; comparatively, a glass of absinthe averaged fifteen centimes, while a bottle of wine was one hundred centimes, or a franc.

A DELICATE TRADITION

An aspect of absinthe that people are drawn to is the ritual of its preparation. Unlike wine or other spirits, one does not typically pour the drink into a glass and consume it. Well, one could, but it's a bitter spirit and is often 70 percent alcohol by volume, so drinking it straight might not be a good idea for a novice.

Absinthe was originally prepared by adding ice water and sugar to the drink at the consumer's discretion. As absinthe became popular among the upper crust, new tools were invented to make absinthe enjoyment more of an experience. A special glass, a slotted spoon, a lump of sugar, and a fountain of ice water were usually used, especially when absinthe was being enjoyed in groups.

Absinthe is poured into a Pontarlier glass, a reservoir glass rounded at the bottom that flares upward. These glasses typically have a bubble or demarcation at the bottom, indicating how much absinthe to use. Next, a specially made slotted spoon is placed onto the glass, with a lump of sugar on it (some people opt for two lumps; it all depends on your taste). Ice water is then slowly dripped from a unique fountain onto the sugar. The process dissolves the sugar into the absinthe and releases the oils of the absinthe's wormwood from their suspension.

As the ice water and sugar are added to the mix, the absinthe changes from a bright green to a cloudy opaque,

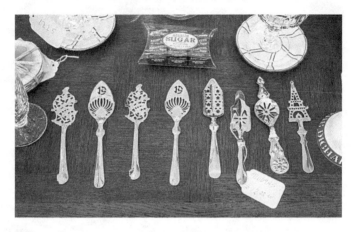

Slotted absinthe spoons, French Antique Shop, New Orleans. Courtesy photographer David Rodrigue.

almost greenish white color, and the absinthe's strength decreases. This transformation is called La Louche, or "the clouding." La Louche results from the ouzo effect—a spontaneous emulsification effect that happens when ice water combines with the chemicals in the absinthe. The result is a libation that is almost glowing. The drink is then gently stirred with the slotted spoon and consumed.

In my research, I learned that another way to prepare absinthe is with a *brouilleur,* a tool used to louche an individual glass of absinthe. This metal or glass device sits on top of a glass of absinthe, dripping a measured amount of water into the glass. One example of *brouilleur* is a *balancier,* which uses a seesaw motion to drip water onto a sugar cube, through an absinthe spoon, and into the absinthe. A *brouilleur* isn't large or bulky like an absinthe fountain, and it is significantly less expensive.

You might be wondering why you wouldn't mix sugared ice water into the absinthe and be done with it. Well, there's no fun in that, but really, the drip fountains full of ice water served a practical purpose. First, ice was hard to come by in the mid-1800s. A small amount of ice could be placed in the drip fountain and cool a large amount of water. Also, the process and ritual of preparing absinthe with the fountain were part of its appeal. After all, most people only consumed one glass of absinthe an evening, so there was no need to rush it. The preparation was integral to the overall experience.

According to bartenders familiar with absinthe, typical absinthe preparation is one part absinthe and three to five parts of water. However, you may prepare it with one part

Absinthe fountain and accessories, French Antique Shop, New Orleans.
Courtesy photographer David Rodrigue.

absinthe and six parts water, which brings the absinthe's
strength down to the same level as wine. You may also mix
absinthe with chilled simple syrup if you don't happen to
have an absinthe fountain on hand.

In my research, I learned that some prepare absinthe by lighting an absinthe-soaked sugar cube on fire. This is not recommended. This "fire method" became popular in the late 1990s. It is strictly for show and does nothing to add to the taste of the absinthe. Not only is an open flame near absinthe dangerous, but according to the Wormwood Society, this process obscures the balance of the botanicals in the drink. A popular phrase in the absinthe community is "Friends don't let friends burn absinthe."

If you're new to the world of absinthe, your best bet might be a simple absinthe cocktail made with other ingredients that will dull the overwhelming anise flavor of the alcohol. Absinthe Suissesse is made with absinthe, almond syrup, cream, and a touch of floral orange blossom water. Death in the Afternoon, invented by Ernest Hemingway and named for his book about Spanish bullfighting, is an absinthe cocktail made with champagne. The Necromancer is made with absinthe, Lillet Blanc, elderflower liqueur, fresh lemon juice, and gin. The Sazerac is made with rye, bitters, and simple syrup and served in a glass coated in absinthe. Finally, the absinthe frappé is a frozen twist on the traditional absinthe preparation invented in New Orleans. See the cocktail guide in chapter 6 of this book for tasty absinthe cocktails you'll want to try.

THE GREEN HOUR
FOR RICH AND POOR

In the latter half of the nineteenth century, the glasses and the spoons used for absinthe became a marker of social class in Europe. While some glasses and slotted spoons were basic in design, wealthier families had spoons custom-made by a silversmith and fountains made of crystal. Like a fine china tea set or a set of crystal wine glasses, having high-end tools for the newest drinking obsession was a mark of the upper class in the 1880s.

Although absinthe by the glass was affordable, only the wealthy could afford a whole bottle of the green drink. The French elite enjoyed the "Green Hour" between five and seven every evening, just before dinner. They would gather in cafés or visit each other's homes and enjoy intellectual conversations over glasses of absinthe.

As the beverage gained in popularity among the elite, it carried with it certain social expectations. For example, it was understood that it would only be consumed at certain times of the day. It was okay to enjoy a bit of absinthe before dinner, as it was seen as an appetite stimulant and a way to unwind at the end of the day. Imbibing absinthe after dinner was considered bad form, although as time went on, consumption of absinthe at any time of day became more acceptable.

A lot of absinthe's appeal lay in its high alcohol volume— it was an easy way to get drunk quickly. When comparing the alcohol content to wine, or any other spirit, absinthe knocks them out of the water (or rather, the glass). In addition, many drank it as a "means to an end," a way to escape the day's troubles.

Nineteenth-century life wasn't easy. People had poverty to contend with, and a lack of modern conveniences, such as electricity and plumbing, made life more difficult. So it makes sense that a good way to pass the time was to drink. It's noteworthy that these two sections of society, the very rich and the very poor, found a common interest in their love of absinthe, though for very different reasons.

It was around this time that the legend of absinthe began to grow. As it gained popularity, stories began to be told of other-worldly experiences and "hallucinations" while consuming the spirit. Absinthe became the drink of artists and writers. Those who wanted to be seen as trendy and in fashion consumed it socially, in groups. Absinthe was the cool new drink on the block, and it seemed like everyone wanted a taste.

CHAPTER TWO

UNDER THE INFLUENCE

ABSINTHE AND ART IN THE
NINETEENTH CENTURY

During the nineteenth century, absinthe was a social drink full of ritual and allure, so it was only natural that it drew in the artistic types, for better or for worse. The nineteenth century was a turning point in the arts across Europe, with artists taking bold chances and pushing against societal norms. Absinthe was at the forefront of the revolution.

* * *

ÉDOUARD MANET AND
THE ABSINTHE DRINKER

Parisian artist Édouard Manet was twenty-six years old when he painted his first major work, *The Absinthe Drinker*—the portrait of a ragpicker and his glass of absinthe. The piece, painted in brown and black, portrays a man named Collardet wrapped in a cloak with a top hat on his head. He's leaning against a wall with a small glass of glowing green absinthe at his side. When Manet presented the portrait to the selection committee of the 1859 Paris Salon, it was immediately rejected as members of the higher elite were starting to push back on the inclusion of absinthe in everyday society. France was seen as a wine country, and absinthe was an attack on a very significant facet of French identity.

Days before he presented *The Absinthe Drinker* to the Paris Salon, Manet invited his mentor and former teacher, Thomas Couture, to view the piece. Couture was horrified at the subject matter—an absinthe drinker portrayed in art was seen as immoral and decadent. In Couture's view, the work served no purpose other than to glamorize absinthe

Édouard Manet, *The Absinthe Drinker*, ca. 1859.

culture. Couture left Manet's studio in a frenzy, and the relationship between the two was over.

THE BURDENS OF
CHARLES BAUDELAIRE

One of Manet's most significant influences was Charles Baudelaire, a French poet, essayist, and art critic. Manet and Baudelaire were close, often meeting socially to sketch or exchange ideas. Baudelaire trusted Manet to look after his personal effects when he traveled, and Manet was inspired by Baudelaire's ability to reject outside criticism. In addition, Baudelaire was progressive for the time, often praising the boldness of Manet's work; he saw Manet's art as cutting-edge.

In his work, Baudelaire craved individualism. In one of his first essays, "On Wine and Hashish," published in 1851, he investigated the psychological effects of wine, hashish, and opium. While he praised wine, he became addicted to opium. His work *Les Paradis artificiels,* published in 1860, described the effects of opium and hashish, drug addiction, and how the influence of drugs could be a detriment to modern man and destroy his life.

Like Manet, Baudelaire also courted controversy in his work. In 1857 he published a book of poems entitled *Les Fleurs du mal—The Flowers of Evil*. The work contained poems that focused on eroticism, death, original sin, and self-hatred; six of the poems were censored for their immorality. In response to the poems, Baudelaire was brought to trial on an immorality charge and fined three hundred francs.

In his poem "Poison," from *Les Fleur du mal,* Baudelaire was surely referring to absinthe when he wrote:

> Neither are worth the drug so strong,
> That you distil from your green eyes,
> Lakes where I see my soul capsize,
> Head downwards and where, in one throng,
> I slake my dreams, and quench my sighs.

His suggestion was that absinthe is more potent than even opium.

Edgar Degas, *L'Absinthe,* 1875–76.

EDGAR DEGAS AND
L'ABSINTHE CONTROVERSY

In 1876 Edgar Degas painted one of his most famous works, *L'Absinthe*. Originally titled *Dans un café*, it depicts a man and a woman sitting in a café. The man, seated to the right, is wearing a hat and coat. The woman, sitting to the left, is formally dressed. A cup of coffee sits in front of him, and a glass of absinthe sits in front of her.

The models for the painting were Ellen Andrée, an actress who also posed for Manet, and Marcellin Desboutin, a fellow painter and etcher who had studied under Couture. The couple looks lethargic, sad, and disconnected from each other; many art critics viewed the work as a commentary on the effects of absinthe on the human spirit.

After an art collector named Henry Hill bought *L'Absinthe*, he lent the piece to a Brighton expedition. The description in the exhibition's catalog titled the work *A Sketch at a French Café* and did not mention the absinthe it portrayed. After the exhibition, the painting was put into storage, where it remained until 1892, when it went up for auction.

Degas was a member of Manet's inner circle, and they often exchanged ideas at Café de Bade, Café Guerbois, and a café in La Nouvelle Athènes where *L'Absinthe* is set. Like Manet's portrayal of an absinthe drinker, Degas's depiction of the couple with their glass of absinthe stirred controversy after it was auctioned and put on display in London.

While the *Glasgow Herald* praised the piece as "a picture showing great power and a superb use of material," many critics hated the painting. It was called ugly; critics noted that the figures looked sickly, and they called the coloring of the work morose. Some went so far as to say that *L'Absinthe* shouldn't be considered a work of art at all.

In 1893 art critic George Moore of the *Speaker* wrote of the piece: "The woman that sits beside the artist was at the Elysée Montmartre until two in the morning, then she went to the Rat Mort and had a soupe aux choux; she lives in the Rue Fontaine, or perhaps the Rue Breda; she did not get up until half-past eleven; then she tied a few soiled petticoats round her, slipped on that peignoir, thrust her feet into those loose morning shoes, and came down to the café to have an absinthe before breakfast. Heavens!—what a slut! A life of idleness and low vice is upon her face; we read there her whole life. The tale is not a pleasant one, but it is a lesson." Years later, Moore regretted his review of the work, declaring that the painting was simply a work of art and not a commentary on French drinking culture.

One art critic, however, was a fan of *L'Absinthe* and of Degas himself. In 1893 D. S. MacColl, a renowned Scottish art critic, who wrote for the *Spectator*, described *L'Absinthe* as "the inexhaustible picture, the one that draws you back, and back again. It set a standard by which too many of the would-be 'decorative' inventions in the exhibition are cruelly judged. It is what they call 'a repulsive subject,' two rather sodden people drinking in a café . . . so does this master of character, of form, of colour, watch till the café table-tops and the mirror and the water-bottle and the drinks and the features yield up to him their mysterious affecting note. The subject, if you like, was repulsive as you would have seen it before Degas made it his. If it appears so still, you may make up your mind that the confusion and affliction from which you suffer are incurable." Today *L'Absinthe* is considered one of Degas's finest works.

PAUL VERLAINE AND ARTHUR RIMBAUD: A MATCH MADE IN HELL

The French poet Paul-Marie Verlaine consumed absinthe with the thought that it made his writing better. However, his love of alcohol, especially absinthe, made him violent. Although he was a wondrous poet who wrote lyrical poems about love and melancholy, he attacked his wife frequently and was known for his vicious temper. He once attacked his elderly mother with a knife because he believed she owed him money, and he shot his close friend and fellow poet Arthur Rimbaud with a revolver. Needless to say, the man wasn't going to be the poster boy for absinthe.

Verlaine prided himself on being closely associated with absinthe to the point that he greeted friends with a cry of "I take sugar with it!" in reference to the green drink—and when he drank, he drank hard. Alphonse Lemerre, a bookseller in the Passage Choiseul, noted that Verlaine never left the bookshop without pausing at a café in the passage for a drink. Lemerre said that Verlaine "drank more than one absinthe, and very often." After losing a series of relatives, including his father, his aunt, and a cousin with whom he was especially close, Verlaine's drinking worsened.

In 1871 Arthur Rimbaud arrived in Paris with not much more than a stack of poems and a dream. He had sent Verlaine some of his poetry, and intrigued by the sixteen-year-old writer, Verlaine sent Rimbaud a one-way ticket to the City of Light and invited the young man to live in his home.

When Rimbaud arrived, Verlaine's seventeen-year-old wife, Mathilde Mauté, was pregnant, but that didn't stop the men from becoming close and developing an intimate relationship. The two began an affair fueled by absinthe, opium, and hashish, which, by today's standards, sounds at best questionable and at worst criminal.

As Verlaine's absinthe abuse increased, so did his abuse of Mathilde, whom he beat regularly and even slashed with a knife. Rimbaud encouraged the behavior, saying that a true man shouldn't cater to domesticity.

The encouragement of domestic violence aside, Rimbaud had other faults. Once at Café du Rat Mort, Rimbaud asked Verlaine and another drinking companion to spread their hands on a table, as Rimbaud would play a game and stab between the men's fingers. Verlaine trusted Rimbaud until his knife slipped and slashed Verlaine's wrist. Furthermore, the den where Rimbaud lived with Verlaine was filthy. He prided himself on the lice that infested his long hair, often throwing handfuls of them at passersby. *Charming.*

According to researcher Vernon Philip Underwood, in 1872 Verlaine left his wife and infant son and ran off to London with Rimbaud. He was put off, however, by the lack of absinthe in the city's cafés. A year later, Rimbaud ended the relationship, and Verlaine fled to Brussels, where he began binge drinking and threatening to commit suicide.

Rimbaud met Verlaine in Brussels, but finally fed up with Verlaine's alcoholism and control over him, Rimbaud made plans to leave him. Verlaine refused to let Rimbaud go and sat in a chair blocking the younger man's exit. Verlaine then pulled out his newly purchased revolver and shot it three times, hitting Rimbaud once in the wrist.

Rimbaud had his wound dressed at Saint-Jean hospital and decided to leave Brussels, and Verlaine, once and for all. However, as Rimbaud was boarding a train to Paris, Verlaine once again drew his revolver and threatened to kill him. Fearing for his life, Rimbaud frantically summoned the police, and Verlaine was arrested.

Verlaine was initially charged with attempted murder, but the charges were reduced to wounding with a firearm after Rimbaud agreed to withdraw the complaint. Verlaine served 555 days in prison, mostly in solitary confinement. After abandoning it for many years, he returned to Catholicism and attempted to turn his life around.

Upon his release from prison, Verlaine lived a quiet life for a while. He swore off absinthe, began teaching French in northern England, and dreamed of living a stable life. He returned to France and began teaching English, but things began to unravel when he started a relationship with a young student named Lucien Létinois, who bore a resemblance to Rimbaud.

After his daily morning classes, Verlaine again began imbibing absinthe with regularity. After losing his teaching job, Verlaine resigned himself to a life ruled by the drink. His health began to fail, and he suffered from diabetes, cirrhosis of the liver, syphilis, cardiac issues, and gonorrhea.

Verlaine's health steadily declined in his final years. In 1895, a year before his death, he wrote in his last significant work, *Confessions:* "This absinthe! What horror, when I think of those days . . . and of time not so remote . . . I repeat in all shame I shall have later to tell of many absurdities (and worse) due to the abuse of this horrible drink; this abuse itself, source of folly and of crime, of idiocies and of shame. The governments should suppress this absinthe, and why not?"

Rimbaud's life following his affair with Verlaine was just as tumultuous. In 1876 he enlisted in the Dutch army, participating in the colonial expansion of Somalia and Abyssinia. He ran guns, dealt in coffee, and was involved in the slave trade. By 1890 his leg had been amputated due to an abscess, and an unknown illness paralyzed him. In the end, he converted to Catholicism and prayed constantly.

He died in November 1891, three weeks before his thirty-seventh birthday. Verlaine did not attend his funeral.

OSCAR WILDE'S ABSINTHE LIFESTYLE

Oscar Wilde met Verlaine in 1883 at Café Vachette in Paris. Wilde was immediately taken with Verlaine's genius but put off by his unkempt appearance and declining health. Wilde was a writer who was taking the literary world by storm, and by 1891 he was living an openly gay life in Paris. In 1895 he was charged with indecent acts, convicted of sodomy, and served two years in prison.

Upon his release, Wilde was shunned and was forced to take the name Sebastian Melmoth and live a life of semi-reclusion. He considered himself a vagabond and began consuming absinthe steadily. As for the effect the drink had on him, Wilde said, "After the first glass, you see things as you wish they were. After the second, you see things as they are not. Finally, you see things as they really are, and that is the most horrible thing in the world."

By 1897 Wilde was experiencing hard times. He was romantically interested in poet Ernest Dowson but was rejected. However, Dowson did take advantage of Wilde's infatuation with him, regularly borrowing money that he wouldn't repay for months. Dowson himself had his struggles with absinthe and drank it to excess; when Dowson died, in February 1900, Wilde was devastated and lost himself in alcohol. He refused to write and lived in a decrepit room at Hotel d'Alsace, only emerging to replenish his absinthe glass at the nearby cafés.

The man who once wrote: "Absinthe has a wonderful color, green. A glass of absinthe is as poetical as anything in the world. What difference is there between a glass of absinthe and a sunset?" had slid into poverty, was rejected by his contemporaries, and was suffering from syphilis, seemingly a common ailment at the time. He was thin and developed noticeable infections due to the disease. Still, he continued consuming absinthe, more than likely to numb himself rather than to derive any sort of pleasure from the drink.

Wilde had an abscess in his ear and suffered delirium due to meningitis. Doctors prescribed morphine, which did little to help, although opium and chloral combined with champagne seemed to do the trick. Noticing his rapid decline, Wilde's friend Robert Ross summoned a priest so that the Anglican-raised Wilde could be baptized as a Catholic and receive last rites. He died on November 30, 1900, at the age of forty-six.

VINCENT VAN GOGH: MADNESS OR ABSINTHE?

The artist most closely associated with absinthe and its influence on nineteenth-century culture is Vincent van Gogh. Van Gogh lived a lonely, solitary life plagued with mental illness and alcoholism. Many historians thought that the Dutch painter might have suffered from glaucoma, cataracts, mania, or epilepsy, which led to the swirling colors in his works. However, this is only speculation.

Vincent van Gogh, *Café Table with Absinthe*, 1887.

Van Gogh drank absinthe obsessively, believing that it made him more creative and was a good influence on his work. One of his paintings, *Café Table with Absinthe,* completed in 1887, depicts a glass of absinthe next to a water carafe.

In 1888, fearful that Paris was making him stagnant, he traveled south to Arles, where he could enjoy the company of prostitutes, imbibe absinthe, and paint. He moved into a room at Carrel hotel and restaurant and then into a room at Café de la Gare. Later that year, he settled into a yellow house, where he would make his studio. In Arles, van Gogh found new life and worked steadily. He wrote his brother Theo regularly, mentioning his love of Arles and the people there who seemed to love absinthe as much as he did.

Van Gogh was hopeful for a new life and was sure that Paris and the excesses there had led to his mental troubles and depression. In *Absinthe: History in a Bottle,* Barnaby Conrad III notes that van Gogh also blamed his genes, writing to Theo, "Our neurosis comes, it's true, from our way of living . . . but it is also fatal inheritance." Considering the van Gogh family had quite a few members end up in various mental wards, Vincent might have been on to something.

By the summer of 1888, van Gogh had grown lonely and started spending more time at cafés with fellow absinthe drinkers. One of his favorite spots, Café de l'Alcazar, was the subject of his painting *Night Café*. The scene depicts a barroom with a pool table in the middle and people seated at tables throughout. The hues of the piece are green and yellow, and the connection to, and influence of, absinthe is hard to deny.

In October 1888 painter Paul Gaugin came and stayed at the yellow house with van Gogh, taking up residence in his guest room for nine weeks. It was at Theo's behest that Gaugin kept Vincent company. Theo, Gaugin's art dealer, agreed to pay Gaugin 150 francs a month to stay at the house, and Gaugin was happy to take Theo up on the offer.

The two artists clashed and regularly fought, especially after van Gogh had been drinking. In one recollection, Gaugin told a story of how, while at a café one evening, van Gogh had thrown a glass of absinthe into Gaugin's face. The following day, van Gogh had little recollection of the incident but chased Gaugin down the street three days later with a razor. When Gaugin stared van Gogh down, the Dutchman retreated into the night. Later that night, van Gogh famously cut off a part of his ear in an attempt to win a prostitute's affection. What a wild time!

Gaugin had wisely spent an evening away from the yellow house and returned to see police covering the property. Gaugin was, understandably, horrified. Originally thought to be dead and lying in his bloody bed, van Gogh had only passed out, leaving Gaugin in shock and packing his bags.

By the beginning of 1889, the incidents with Gaugin and the prostitute were all but forgotten, with van Gogh writing in a letter to Theo, "They told me that in this country things like that are not out of the ordinary." However, by early February, van Gogh was admitted to an asylum, complaining of voices in his head and the belief that he was being poisoned.

Once van Gogh was released, he found that people in the city where he had once found sanctuary were cruel to him. He was openly mocked and laughed at; children threw rocks at him. Eighty townspeople signed a petition demanding that van Gogh be permanently institutionalized. The treatment broke van Gogh's heart, and he, once again, felt forlorn and desolate. Vincent wrote Theo that he had no friends and was contemplating suicide, although he thought he lacked the nerve to go through with it.

After a visit from painter Paul Signac, who reported to Theo that van Gogh was drowning himself in absinthe and brandy, van Gogh attempted suicide by drinking a quart of turpentine. He survived the attempt but was again committed to an asylum in May 1889. Medicine being what it was at the time, doctors had trouble diagnosing what had led van Gogh to despair. He was treated for mania, and it was possible that he suffered from syphilis and perhaps a brain lesion, but those are only theories.

By July 27, 1890, long-suffering van Gogh had reached the end of his rope. He could tell his mental facilities were failing him, and he ended his life by shooting himself in the gut. Two days later, he died, at the age of thirty-seven. In a letter obtained by the Van Gogh Museum, Theo, who was with his brother when he died, wrote to his wife, "One of his last words was, 'This is how I wanted to go,' and it took a few moments and then it was over and he found the peace he hadn't been able to find on earth."

Six months later, on January 25, 1891, thirty-three-year-old Theo followed Vincent in death. The cause was listed as "dementia paralytica caused by heredity, chronic disease, overwork, and sadness."

EDGAR ALLAN POE: THE ABSINTHE DRINKER WHO WASN'T?

An American writer who was rumored to have enjoyed absinthe was Edgar Allan Poe, although there is no evidence to that effect. The story probably originated, in part, from Baudelaire's obsession with him. Baudelaire translated Poe's works from 1852 to 1865 and identified with him as both a writer and a person. It's understandable—the two men both lived in poverty and seemingly struggled with addiction. Perhaps it was wishful thinking on Baudelaire's part that someone with whom he identified so closely also enjoyed a good glass of absinthe. However, there is no proof that Poe drank absinthe or even knew what it was.

Although Poe was known to enjoy a drink and maybe even drank to excess at times, he would also go long periods without drinking. As for Poe's absinthe consumption, the Virtual Absinthe Museum says that it's a myth. Although absinthe was advertised in Boston papers as early as 1818 and in Baltimore in 1826, there's no record that Poe drank it or that it influenced his work. If Poe did ever drink absinthe, he probably didn't consume it with any frequency. It's a romantic notion, the idea of Poe writing "The Raven" by candlelight, a glass of absinthe at his side, but in this case, the story is most likely fiction.

CHAPTER THREE

A NEW WORLD

ABSINTHE IN NEW ORLEANS, THE OLD ABSINTHE HOUSE, AND THE ABSINTHE FRAPPÉ

Since the French had fallen so in love with absinthe, it's only natural that it made its way to New Orleans. New Orleans was, after all, a French city; many citizens here spoke French and held loyalties to the country. New Orleanians felt a connection to the people of Paris and their habits.

As in France, the people of New Orleans loved their wine but enjoyed other libations as well. There's evidence that absinthe was in New Orleans as soon as the early 1830s, and advertisements for what was called "absynthe" date back to 1837. With its loose rules, mysterious scene, and European influences, New Orleans became the place to be for those who wanted to enjoy absinthe on this side of the pond.

Shortly after the United States purchased New Orleans, the city began to develop a reputation. It became notorious for attracting questionable types such as prostitutes, thieves, gamblers, bar owners, and those looking for a quick, easy buck. In the early nineteenth century, New Orleans's population started to increase despite this reputation or maybe because of it.

By 1820 New Orleans was changing; the census reports that twenty-nine thousand people lived in the city, among them were free Blacks, enslaved people, foreigners, and a white population. According to Doris Lanier's book, *Absinthe, The Cocaine of the Nineteenth Century,* by 1836 New Orleans's population numbers had soared to sixty thousand. There were 543 licensed drinking establishments in the city, and many of them sold liquor without the benefit of a license. There were also over 500 gambling houses and multiple brothels.

New Orleans was seen as a city of decadence where one could come and, theoretically, leave their morals at home. Revelry was considered a part of the lifestyle, and drinking and drunkenness were regular occurrences that didn't carry the "shame" that they would have in other cities. Like it or not, the young city of New Orleans was making a name for itself.

HUMBLE BEGINNINGS

One bar not only served absinthe but became famous for it. Built in 1806, the Old Absinthe House's location started as an importing and commission business owned by Pedro Font and Francisco Juncadella. From this building at 240 Bourbon Street, they imported food, wine, and goods from Spain, their native country.

Absinthe historian Ray Bordelon explained that in August 1820, Juncadella died and left all of his possessions, including the building at 240 Bourbon Street, to his widow, Doña Rosa. Upon Juncadella's death, Doña Rosa, a shrewd businesswoman, hired a notary and had her late husband's succession appraised. The notary spent four days going through everything that Francisco had owned in life, including bottles, casks, pipes, tobacco, and properties. When all was said and done, the sum came to a tidy $36,873. Half of that fortune went to Doña Rosa and her daughters, Françoise and Emerée, and the other half went to Francisco's business partner, Pedro Font.

Juncadella hoped that Font would carry on his business after his death. However, Font and his family soon returned to Spain, and Doña Rosa left the property in the hands of her nephew, Jacinto Aleix.

At this point in its history, the building for the Old Absinthe House had gone through a few incarnations. The bottom floor was set up as a liquid refreshment stop around 1815. A 1933 record states that a bar was operating there as early as 1826. The top floor operated as many different businesses—in 1838 it was a shoe shop and then served as a grocery store. In 1843, under Jacinto Aleix's ownership, the building was converted to a public house called Aleix's Coffee House. Like *café* in Europe, *coffeehouse* was another name for a drinking establishment or bar.

In 1861 Jacinto Aleix died, leaving the charge of the Coffee House to his widow, Maria Severine Aleix, and sons, Eduardo, Leopold, and Pierre Oscar Aleix. By 1865 Leopold Aleix was running the basement bar at the French Opera House. When Leopold's lease at the Opera House ended, his brother Pierre Oscar took over the lease from 1866 to 1868.

Located at the corner of Bourbon and Toulouse Streets in the French Quarter, the French Opera House's three-story building had become a New Orleans social hub. When the Aleixes' lease ended on the bar there, they parted ways with the establishment. However, there was one person at the French Opera House whom the brothers weren't ready to leave behind.

THE HOUSE THAT ABSINTHE BUILT

In 1869 the Aleix brothers hired Cayetano Ferrér, a bartender from Barcelona, to tend bar at the Coffee House. New Orleans is a drinking town, and Ferrér already had a reputation for mixing some of the tastiest drinks this side of the Mississippi River.

According to Bordelon, Ferrér had an interesting history. He briefly served in the Confederate army toward the end of the Civil War. He worked at a sawmill in Jefferson, Louisiana, and at a grocery store in Algiers, Louisiana. Finally, he found himself serving drinks at the basement bar of the French Opera House, before settling in at Aleix's Coffee House.

By 1874 Ferrér had taken over the Aleix building's lease and renamed the spot "Absinthe Room." Perhaps it was because he was from Spain and knew the allure that absinthe seemed to have on the drinking kind in Europe, but the Absinthe Room quickly became known as the place to be in the city of New Orleans. Although absinthe was served in places like Chicago, New York, and San Francisco, New

Orleans became known as the absinthe epicenter of the United States through the nineteenth century.

This place, serving this mysterious green drink from green marble fountains imported from Europe that sat right on the bar top, got people talking. Receipts suggest that in 1871 Maria Aleix had purchased the fountains, along with four cases of absinthe, bar fixtures, and other accoutrements, from a saloon owner, for a little over two thousand dollars. The purchase proved to be a good investment. Ferrér would prepare the absinthe at his bar in the French style with water dripped slowly from the fountains, sugar added, and the mixture stirred until properly louched.

Interestingly, the absinthe spoon was a popular accessory not commonly used in absinthe preparation in the United States. Bordelon explained that in France and other parts of Europe, it was typical for the bartender to serve absinthe in a glass and water in a decanter to allow the customer to prepare the drink themselves, adding sugar to their liking via the absinthe spoon. However, in the United States, the bartender typically prepared the absinthe for the customer.

Absinthe was a social drink, and the Absinthe Room became the place where the most progressive of society came to swap ideas and be seen. The Absinthe Room became so popular that Ferrér enlisted the help of his family to work at the place and serve customers. Ferrér's mother, father, and sons, Felix, Paul, and Jacinto, all attended to the needs of a crowd that had developed a thirst for absinthe. In addition to being known for his absinthe, Ferrér's Absinthe Room was also the place to get "good liquors and Spanish wines," as Ferrér himself put it in an 1882 ad that is a part of Bordelon's collection.

A REFRESHING FRAPPÉ

In 1874 Ferrér concocted a refreshing twist on regular absinthe. Bordelon explained that the drink that would come to be known as the absinthe frappé was prepared when absinthe, cold water, and sugar were combined in a glass.

Ice was added to the mix, and it was stirred with a long, twist-handled bar spoon until the cocktail was icy. Simple syrup and soda water might have been used in an original drink variation; it was all a matter of preference.

Frappé is a term for any drink that is mixed and combined with ice until very cold. Ice is added to a shaker full of cocktail ingredients, and the mix is shaken or vigorously stirred until frost forms on the outside of the shaker. These days a frappé can refer to any drink served cold or blended with ice such as a margarita, a daiquiri, or even coffee. The definition is very loose, but for these purposes, it simply means an ice-cold drink.

Herbsaint frappé, Old Absinthe House, New Orleans. Courtesy photographer David Rodrigue.

Absinthe frappé, Pirate's Alley Café, New Orleans. Courtesy photographer David Rodrigue.

Absinthe frappé, Mr. B's Bistro, New Orleans. Courtesy photographer David Rodrigue.

Absinthe frappé, Hermes Bar, New Orleans. Courtesy photographer David Rodrigue.

The more modern absinthe frappé is made with absinthe, simple syrup, and soda water shaken together and served over crushed ice. Mint is sometimes muddled into the drink or added as a garnish. Some versions use all of the traditional ingredients, along with an egg white, and serve it in a cocktail glass with no ice.

As the story goes, Ferrér had the idea to create a version of an absinthe drink that someone could enjoy in the morning. The combination of the water and ice reduces the "punch" of regular absinthe that one might enjoy later in the day. Also, because the drink is served very cold, it was the perfect way to cool off on a hot New Orleans day. Without the benefit of air-conditioning, a cold drink goes a long way toward making someone feel comfortable.

In 1886 the Absinthe Room became the "Old Absinthe Room," and when Cayetano Ferrér died, his widow, Marguerite, and his sons carried on the business and continued to serve the frappé that so many had grown to love. In 1890 the business changed its name to "Old Absinthe House," which it is known as today. Although the bar suffered bankruptcy in 1902, the Ferrér family continued to run the Old Absinthe House until 1914.

By 1904 people were so infatuated with the absinthe frappé that Victor Herbert and Glen MacDonough wrote a song for the musical *It Happened in Nordland* about the cocktail. Aptly named "Absinthe Frappé," the song was famous for its time:

Absinthe frappé, Cure, New Orleans. Courtesy photographer David Rodrigue.

When life seems gray and dark the dawn and you are blue

There is they say on such a morn one thing to do

Rise up and ring, a bellboy call to you straight way

And bid him bring a cold and tall absinthe frappé

It will free you first from the burning thirst

That is born of a night of the bowl

Like a sun 'twill rise through the inky skies

That so heavily hang o'er your soul

At the first cool sip on your fevered lip

You determine to live through the day

Life's again worthwhile as with dawning smile

You imbibe your absinthe frappé

The deed is done so waste no woe o'er yestereen

Nor swear to shun a year or so the festive scene

Remorse will pass despair will fade with speed away

Before a glass of rightly made absinthe frappé

A PLACE OF LEGEND

It wasn't all great times at what would be the Old Absinthe House. According to Bordelon, in 1851 there was an anti-

Spanish movement in New Orleans, and the Absinthe Room fell prey to vandals. One night, a mob broke into the bar by taking axes to its doors. The group destroyed liquor bottles and mirrors and threw the bar's furniture out into the street. Ferrér sued the city of New Orleans for failing to protect his property, but he lost when the case went to court.

In 1918 writer Aleister Crowley was so inspired by New Orleans and the Old Absinthe House that he wrote "Absinthe: The Green Goddess" about the place. He then pinned the essay on the bar's walls.

In the composition, he wrote in part: "For I am no longer in the city accursed, where Time is horsed on the white gelding Death, his spurs rusted with blood. There is a corner of the United States which he has overlooked. It lies in New Orleans, between Canal Street and Esplanade Avenue; the Mississippi for its base. Thence it reaches northward to a most curious desert land, where is a cemetery lovely beyond dreams. Its walls low and whitewashed, within which straggles a wilderness of strange and fantastic tombs; and hard by is that great city of brothels which is so cynically mirthful a neighbor. Art is the soul of life and the Old Absinthe House is heart and soul of the old quarter of New Orleans."

In the early twentieth century, interesting times were coming for New Orleans, the Old Absinthe House, and all those who enjoyed absinthe and alcohol. A ban on absinthe was on the horizon, and Prohibition wasn't far behind. So, what would all of this mean for a city that enjoys a good cocktail and isn't big on following the rules?

CHAPTER FOUR

GOOD TIMES NEVER LAST

THE GREAT ABSINTHE BAN

Does absinthe cause hallucinations? The short answer is no.

Imagine that you're in a café in the nineteenth century and you order a glass of wine. You're a wine drinker, so you gulp the wine down and enjoy it. Maybe you're enjoying the evening, and you decide to have another glass of wine—no problem. Wine is only about 7 to 11 percent alcohol and certainly not strong enough to cause any strange effects.

Now imagine you're in the same café in the middle of the wine crisis. A pesky aphid is eviscerating the wine fields, so the supply is short. You decide to try something different; you decide to try absinthe. You have one, and you enjoy it; it's a bit bitter, but a little sugar makes it go down easily. You decide to have another absinthe—here's where the trouble starts. The absinthe you're drinking is 120 to 144 proof, or 60 to 72 percent alcohol. It stands to reason that if you gulp one or two down, you might start seeing things. There's nothing out of the ordinary in the drink—just a lot of alcohol. No, you aren't hallucinating; you're drunk!

THE SCIENCE BEHIND ABSINTHE AND THE RUMOR

From the beginning, there seemed to be some pushback on absinthe and its effects. Because it was a reasonably new spirit, questions were raised about how it affected the human body and mind and influenced behaviors. There was talk that if someone drank too much absinthe, they went mad. As explained by Barnaby Conrad III, in the late nineteenth century, renowned French psychiatrist Dr. Valentin Magnan believed absinthe led to mental illness and a decline in French culture. He began experimenting with alcohol and absinthe and studying its effects on guinea pigs, cats, and rabbits.

In one experiment, as described in an 1869 issue of the *Lancet*, a guinea pig was placed in a glass case with a saucer of wormwood oil. Another was placed in a glass case with pure alcohol. Magnan observed that the guinea pig that inhaled the wormwood vapors began experiencing epileptiform convulsions, while the guinea pig that inhaled the alcohol vapors simply became drunk.

In another experiment, Magnan gave dogs large amounts of alcohol, which caused them to hallucinate and die. He noted, however, that these animals did not experience any convulsions. Instead, he observed that when he gave the animals even small doses of absinthe, they experienced epileptic-like seizures; larger quantities of absinthe produced more significant episodes.

Furthermore, Magnan studied 250 people who were suffering from acute alcoholism. He concluded that while a typical alcoholic suffered from delirium tremens, people who regularly consumed absinthe were prone to absinthe-induced epilepsy, likely caused by lesions on the brain tissue. Magnan thought that thujone, an essence found in wormwood, absinthe's primary ingredient, was to blame. He suggested that long-term consumption of absinthe containing wormwood would lead to convulsions, hallucinations, seizures, amnesia, and violence.

After Magnan published his findings, many were skeptical of the accuracy of his experiments. Some argued that there is a difference between a small animal inhaling pure wormwood oil and a human consuming a drink containing trace amounts of wormwood. However, Magnan doubled down on his claims and stated that the worst alcoholics he encountered in Parisian hospitals were absinthe drinkers, and he believed that that the drink would lead to the downfall of France.

Today one might argue that while consuming highly concentrated amounts of pure wormwood oil has deleterious effects on the brain, absinthe itself doesn't contain thujone in those large amounts. Yet Magnan believed that thujone, and absinthe itself, leads the person who consumes it to madness.

Thujone is a gamma-aminobutyric acid (GABA) inhibitor; it blocks the neurotransmitter's receptors in the brain. If consumed in large amounts, thujone can cause seizures; however, after the distillation process, only a small amount of the compound is left in absinthe—certainly not enough to cause any harm. Needless to say, the alcohol in absinthe will get you long before the thujone does.

Scientific studies aside, it's likely that because absinthe was so high in alcohol, it was simply causing thoughts of delusions in those who were consuming it. These effects would be present especially if the absinthe weren't diluted with ice water. As someone was drinking absinthe over a period of time, the high levels of alcohol played tricks on the mind, leading the consumer to believe they were experiencing mental euphoria when, in fact, they were just very drunk.

Furthermore, as absinthe gained in popularity, many factories began producing low-grade, cheap absinthe. This absinthe contained harmful chemicals such as copper sulfate and antimony trichloride, which lead to copper toxicity and antimony poisoning. These chemicals are what caused hallucinations and not thujone, as Magnan claimed.

THE WINEMAKERS' CASE
AGAINST ABSINTHE

Phil Baker explains in *The Book of Absinthe* that by the 1870s, French winemakers were starting to get nervous, and with good reason. Phylloxera, that aphid we learned about in chapter 1, was ravaging their wine crops. As a result, wine production slowed, and the people of France began replacing their favorite wine with absinthe. The winemakers saw trouble, and they knew that something had to be done to nip this absinthe infatuation in the bud.

To draw interest back in their direction, French winemakers put their collective weight behind France's temperance movement. They argued that wine did not contribute to alcoholism but that industrial alcohol, such as absinthe, did. They claimed that it wasn't until the wine shortages that the people of France began overindulging in alcohol. The winemakers painted wine as pure because it was fermented; distilled liquor was seen as the root of France's problems.

Furthermore, absinthe was seen as toxic, and all of society's ills could supposedly be traced back to the drink. Studies had shown, allegedly, that consuming large amounts of absinthe could lead someone to delusions. Thus, what was once an innocent spirit to be enjoyed before dinner was now labeled a detriment to French society. The case against absinthe was gaining momentum; it just needed one notable event to put it over the top.

ENTER JEAN LANFRAY

As described in Conrad's *Absinthe: History in a Bottle,* one August morning in 1905, Jean Lanfray of Vaud, Switzerland, got up for work and started his day with a couple of shots of absinthe. As his wife, who was four months pregnant, cooked breakfast, Lanfray asked her to wax his boots.

She shrugged off the request, and Lanfray went out to tend to the cows. At five thirty that morning, Lanfray enjoyed coffee, brandy, crème de menthe, and cognac mixed with soda. At lunch, he imbibed seven glasses of wine and ended his workday with coffee and a shot of brandy. Lanfray was already nicely drunk when he returned home and consumed a liter of wine with his father. He ended his evening with another coffee and brandy.

When Lanfray noticed that his wife hadn't waxed his boots, as he had asked, a fight ensued. The couple exchanged words, and Lanfray became enraged. He got his Vetterli rifle, with a magazine that held twelve cartridges, from the closet. Lanfray then aimed the gun at his wife and pulled the trigger, killing her instantly. When his four-year-old daughter, Rose, appeared in the doorway, he shot her in the chest, killing her. Lanfray then entered the room of his two-year-old daughter, Blanche, and shot her to death in her crib.

Lanfray then held the unwieldy weapon to his temple but was unable to pull the trigger. He attempted to tie a piece of string to the trigger and pull it that way; that only resulted in Lanfray shooting himself in his jaw. In his bloody and disoriented state, Lanfray cradled the body of his dead daughter Blanche, stumbled into his yard, and fell into a deep sleep.

When authorities brought him to see the bodies of his slain family, Lanfray had no memory of what he had done. An immediate investigation into Lanfray's drinking habits began. Authorities learned that on the day of the murders, he had consumed wine, brandy, and two glasses of absinthe.

That was all the local newspapers needed to hear—the fact that Lanfray had consumed massive amounts of wine on the day he killed his family was inconsequential. The Lanfray murders were caused by absinthe, and something had to be done about it. Within weeks, a petition was signed by 34,375 men and 48,075 women, demanding the immediate ban of absinthe.

At Lanfray's trial, a Swiss psychiatrist, Dr. Albert Mahaim, testified that the murders resulted from absinthe madness, or absinthism. The doctor concluded that Lanfray's regular consumption of absinthe had driven him to madness and to brutally murder his family. As a result, Lanfray was convicted of quadruple murder and sentenced to thirty years in prison. He hung himself in his cell three days later.

THE BAN GAINS MOMENTUM

Whether absinthe had anything to do with the Lanfray murders or not, the damage had already been done: absinthe was dangerous, and it had to go. In May 1906 the Vaud legislature voted to ban absinthe. A similar incident in Geneva, Switzerland, in which a man was said to have murdered his wife after an absinthe binge, didn't help matters; the push for a complete absinthe ban was swift.

To satiate the masses but keep the money from absinthe flowing, politicians suggested that café owners have a special license to sell it or allow it to be regulated by the government and produce a higher grade of absinthe. They tried arguing that regulating it in this way would result in a healthier product.

Now it was the absinthe makers who were getting nervous. The Pernod distillery and other factories, such as

Duval and Cusenier, were making millions in the absinthe business, and the thought of a complete absinthe ban promised to have devastating financial consequences.

The absinthe makers tried to argue that a ban on absinthe was a strike against industry liberties, but it was all for naught. A popular vote was held, and absinthe lost, 23,062 to 16,025. Absinthe makers continued to argue that a ban was an infringement on industry rights, but the odds were not in their favor.

Between the medical experiments, the temperance movement, and domestic murder blamed on absinthe, the drink didn't stand a chance in the court of public opinion. In February 1907 the Grand Conseil banned the sale of absinthe and all absinthe imitations, and in July 1908 article 32 was added to the federal constitution prohibiting absinthe in Switzerland. On October 7, 1910, absinthe was legally banned in Switzerland—this was considered a victory for the country's morality. Holland followed suit and banned absinthe, also in 1910. The United States banned it in 1912; the ban here received little to no resistance because the United States only imported twenty-five thousand cases of absinthe a year. Belgium had already banned absinthe by 1905.

The party might have been over in Switzerland, but absinthe was still consumed with enthusiasm in France. By 1910 the French were drinking over thirty-six million liters of the stuff a year. Once again, absinthe was seen as the country's favorite drink, and once again, the winemakers were nervous.

Realistically speaking, the winemakers had no reason to feel threatened by the popularity of absinthe. Wine still accounted for 72 percent of alcohol consumed in the country, while absinthe accounted for only 3 percent. Yet soon enough, there started to be a push against absinthe in Paris, with politicians raising concerns about the nation's very future, especially if absinthe indulgence continued with such vigor.

In 1914 France was on the precipice of World War I, when the minister of the interior, Louis Malvy, requested that the sale of absinthe be banned in France. The ban was applauded as politicians declared that France had been saved from the lunacy and evils of the drink. Monsieur Adolphe

Girod, deputy of Pontarlier, argued that high-end absinthe was never the villain in the story. In reality, it was cheap knock-off or homemade absinthe that caused the illusion of absinthism in France. On March 4, 1915, the Chamber of Deputies voted to ban the production and sale of absinthe in France, and the law went into effect twelve days later.

Two weeks after the French ban, farmers were forced to burn their wormwood crops without reimbursement. Distillers had three million liters of absinthe seized and were paid a base price for the stuff. Factories were shut down, and thousands lost their jobs; many of the men who toiled in the factories went off to war, never to return. According to absinthe expert Theodore Breaux, the Pernod Fils distillery closed its doors in 1915. The space that the distillery occupied became a field hospital during the First World War and was later destroyed.

There was still a way to get absinthe in Europe, however. The United Kingdom and Spain never banned absinthe; it had never been particularly trendy in the United Kingdom. At this time, forms of absinthe continued to be produced in Spain, Portugal, and what is now the Czech Republic.

However, absinthe aficionados considered the product of inferior quality to what had been produced in France in the nineteenth century.

PROHIBITION IN THE UNITED STATES

It seemed, in the United States, that the banning of absinthe was only the beginning. In November 1918 the United States Congress passed the Wartime Prohibition Act, which banned the sale of alcoholic drinks that contained an alcohol content of 1.28 percent or greater. The act took effect in June 1919.

Total prohibition was proposed as the Eighteenth Amendment in December 1917, it was approved and ratified as part of the Constitution in January 1919, and it was officially enforced as of January 1920. The Volstead Act, the formal name of the National Prohibition Act, prohibited the manufacture, transport, and sale of alcohol, although it was difficult to enforce such a law.

Tenacious New Orleanians, who refused to be swayed

by the new laws, kept their drinking habits as usual, even if they were a bit more discreet. Illegal liquor was smuggled into the city via Lake Pontchartrain, while other citizens made their alcohol at home.

Speakeasies were relatively commonplace and easy to find if you knew where to look. Taxi drivers peddled bottles of booze out of their cabs, while restaurant waiters sold drinks from hidden flasks.

Raids were a part of Prohibition life. Illegal alcohol was confiscated, the offending businesses were fined, and some were closed, but the locals remained unfazed for the most part.

NEW ORLEANS HAS A PLAN

Prohibition was no match for the Old Absinthe House. At this point, the bar at the corner of Bourbon and Bienville had been operating with great success for eighty years. Its newest owner, Pierre Cazebonne, had owned the bar since 1914, after buying it from the Ferrér family.

The Sazerac Bar and Henry Ramos's Stag Café, two other notable bars in town, tried their best to work around the rules of Prohibition but failed. The Sazerac Bar secretly served liquor for a bit, but it was busted and went back to operating as an oyster bar. Henry Ramos quit his bar's lease and auctioned off the bar's contents, including the bar's fixtures, mahogany counters, oil paintings, and art glass canopy.

In *The Belle Époque Guide to Absinthe,* author Laura Bellucci explains that despite the laws, Cazebonne continued selling liquor under the guise of operating his business as a restaurant and later as a soda fountain. He was raided and fined, of course, but Cazebonne kept changing the name of his bar and running it as usual—that is, until 1926, when the authorities put a padlock on the door of 240 Bourbon Street, seemingly shutting down the operation for good, or at least for a year.

By 1928 authorities finally unlocked the bar, and the building's lease was signed over to the Vieux Carré Association. Jacinto Ferrér, son of Cayetano Ferrér, bartended at the Old Absinthe House and lived upstairs from the es-

A sign at the Old Absinthe House advertises an absinthe frappé. Courtesy photographer David Rodrigue.

tablishment; he attempted to sell the contents of the bar—fixtures, absinthe fountains, and other paraphernalia—to the Vieux Carré Association.

But as soon as the padlock was off of the door of the Old Absinthe House, Cazebonne made his move. He claimed the fixtures and contents of the bar by his right of sale from Felix Ferrér in 1914 and moved all of the contents just down the street to 400 Bourbon Street, the location of a soda shop Cazebonne had wisely purchased.

The switch was made, and bootleg liquor was, once again, being served on the Old Absinthe's famed bar top. Perhaps, however, Cazebonne had gotten too cocky—this location of the "Absinthe House Bar," as it was now known, was shut down when the slick and determined owner placed a sign out front notifying neighbors of his business.

In 1933 Prohibition was repealed. The Old Absinthe Bar, as Cazebonne now called it, was operating business as usual in its new spot at 400 Bourbon Street. It would operate there until 2004, when it moved back to its rightful place at 240 Bourbon Street.

ABSINTHE MINUS THE SIN

After Prohibition was repealed, absinthe was still banned in the United States and other European countries. However, that didn't stop people from craving something with that unique anise flavor. As a result, quite a few anise-flavored liqueurs began to be used in place of absinthe in cocktails.

Pastis is an anise-flavored spirit that derives its licorice flavor from star anise and licorice root rather than green anise and fennel. It has a lower alcohol by volume (ABV) level than absinthe and is typically bottled with sugar. Paul Ricard created Ricard Pastis in 1932 and marketed it as "true pastis from Marseille." Ouzo is a Greek liquor, often made with anise, and was also used as an absinthe replacement; however, people who had previously enjoyed absinthe in their cocktails felt like something was missing.

New Orleanians J. Marion Legendre and Reginald Parker were serving in World War I in France when they learned how to make absinthe. Although absinthe was banned at the time, they had the idea to produce the same product without the controversial herb grande wormwood.

Created in 1934, the product was initially made under the name "Legendre Absinthe," although it was merely an absinthe substitute. The Federal Alcohol Control Administration objected to the use of the word *absinthe* in the drink's name, so it was changed to "Legendre Herbsaint," or "Sacred Herb." Legendre and Parker created the closest possible legal substitute for absinthe, and cocktail lovers rejoiced.

Herbsaint frappé, Columns hotel, New Orleans. Photograph by the author.

In June 1949 the Sazerac Company bought J. M. Legendre & Company and eventually reduced the proof of the spirit from 120 to 90. In December 2009 the Sazerac Company reintroduced J. M. Legendre's original 100 proof recipe as "Herbsaint Original," which is still on the market today.

Although the absinthe ban was eventually lifted, the popularity of Herbsaint and Herbsaint cocktails has not dwindled. At the Old Absinthe House, you can enjoy an Herbsaint frappé made in the same style as a traditional absinthe frappé, simply substituting absinthe for Herbsaint.

Some other popular cocktails made with Herbsaint are Cocktail à la Louisiane made with rye, Benedictine, sweet vermouth, Peychaud's bitters, and Herbsaint; and the Zombie, which contains Herbsaint, rum, grenadine, and bitters.

The absinthe ban in the United States would last until 2007, when a New Orleanian, armed with science, set out to prove that absinthe's reputation as a dangerous liquor was unfair and unfounded.

CHAPTER FIVE

ANOTHER ROUND

THE BAN IS LIFTED, AND ABSINTHE
FINDS A SECOND LIFE

In 2007 the regulations on absinthe changed. Modern science proved that the levels of thujone in absinthe were safe and that it could, once again, be sold legally in the United States. To explain how we got here, you have to start with a man named Theodore Breaux. Breaux is a New Orleanian, absinthe expert, chemist, and microbiologist who used science to prove absinthe's reputation as a dangerous drink was unfounded.

THEODORE BREAUX:
SCIENCE AND ABSINTHE

Theodore Breaux first became interested in absinthe in 1993, after reading a book on the subject. Fascinated, he began researching absinthe, what made it so "dangerous," and what made it so special.

In 1996 the stars aligned when Breaux got a call from a New Orleans antique shop willing to sell him a bottle of early Pernod Tarragona absinthe for three hundred dollars. From there, a colleague connected him with a bottle of unopened Édouard Pernod export-strength absinthe that was nearly one hundred years old. Breaux refers to these bottles as the Rosetta Stone in his journey of absinthe research.

Because Breaux is a scientist, he wanted to know what was in vintage absinthe. In June 2000 he became the first person to analyze samples of vintage absinthe using modern science; he conducted tests that couldn't have been done when absinthe was initially banned.

His analysis revealed that the vintage absinthe was high in alcohol volume and contained thujone levels between zero and forty-eight parts per million. The thujone levels in the vintage absinthe were not considered harmful, and there was nothing in this absinthe that should have led to its ban. As Breaux explained, as long as absinthe is produced responsibly, there's nothing wrong with it.

During Breaux's absinthe journey, he discovered that public interest in absinthe in places like the Czech Republic had led to a market full of fake absinthes that were nothing more than liquor that had been dyed green. These products held no resemblance to real absinthe. While determined to create a spirit as close to nineteenth-century absinthe as possible, Breaux spent time in France.

Breaux founded Jade Liqueurs in 2000, and in 2004 he began producing absinthe that is as close to the absinthe that Verlaine and van Gogh drank as you can get. The herbs and botanicals for Breaux's Jade Liqueurs absinthes are grown in the same place as herbs grown for absinthe in the nineteenth century.

He produces his absinthe in France at the Combier Distillery, using equipment that dates back to the nineteenth century, including two large stills from the defunct

Pernod Fils distillery. Breaux wants his absinthe to be as authentic as possible, down to every detail—from its distillation to its bottling and labels. Because of his exhaustive research and passion for absinthe, Breaux's Jade Liqueurs is considered the gold standard for modern-day absinthe.

THE PROCESS OF LIFTING
THE REGULATIONS ON ABSINTHE

In 2003 the process of legalizing absinthe in the United States was beginning to take shape. A Texas-based alcohol beverage importer, Dan Dotson, asked to seek approval for Kübler Absinthe, a Swiss brand, to be imported into the United States. In 2004 Kübler submitted absinthe samples to the Alcohol and Tobacco Tax and Trade Bureau's (TTB) laboratory.

According to the Virtual Absinthe Museum and Robert C. Lehrman, of Lehrman Beverage Law, PLLC, the law firm that assisted Kübler in its negotiations with the TTB and the FDA, analysis proved that Kübler Absinthe contained ten parts per million or less of thujone—the legal limit in the United States; TTB confirmed that the product was safe.

TTB also determined that the formula for the absinthe would not have to be altered in any way to obtain "legal" status. However, TTB would not allow the product to be labeled as "absinthe," which the bureau considered an illegal drug term. For a product that has been named Kübler Absinthe since 1863, this posed a bit of a problem.

Labeling a product as absinthe is tricky because, as Breaux explained, there is no legal definition of *absinthe* in the United States; it is not a legally recognized category. Therefore, anything can be bottled and called absinthe, regardless of whether it's the real thing or not.

In 2007 the argument over using the word *absinthe* on product labels was in the courts. In desperation, the law firm handling the case turned to the Swiss Embassy for help. The embassy's representative explained that absinthe is legal in Switzerland and had been since 2005; labeling the product as absinthe is not harmful. In addition, the embassy representative stated that Kübler Absinthe is a fine product made by a reputable company and there is no reason that the proper labeling shouldn't be approved.

TTB finally approved the use of the word *absinthe* on the product's label, as long as it was not the same size or larger than the brand's name. In addition to the labeling, the FDA said that the thujone content in any absinthe sold in the United States must not be higher than ten parts per million. This wasn't an issue because ten parts per million is considered well within the normal range for thujone in absinthe.

Around this same time, in 2006, Viridian Spirits was doing its own work to legalize absinthe in the United States. The company argued that its absinthe, Lucid, created by Theodore Breaux, was safe and should be permitted to be shipped and sold in the United States. However, TTB took issue with the product being labeled as absinthe, as it had in the Kübler case.

To prove that absinthe should be sold legally, Vince O'Brien, the lawyer for Viridian Spirits, and the Viridian team clarified the true reason for the original absinthe bans. They explained how the winemakers in nineteenth-century France had seen absinthe as a threat and had pushed for it to be banned under the false narrative that it was dangerous.

Breaux made a statement arguing that there was no rule, regulation, or law that prevented a product from being labeled absinthe. The legal team also stated that the 1912 Food Inspection Decision that had banned absinthe had been repealed in 1938 by the creation of the FDA, and, they argued, it wasn't enforceable even before 1938.

After a lengthy debate over Lucid's labeling and its use of the word *absinthe,* both TTB and the Viridian team agreed that rather than just labeling the product "Lucid Absinthe," adding the word *Supérieure,* French for "superior," to the label was a good compromise. As a result, on March 5, 2007, Lucid Absinthe Supérieure received its certificate of label approval and became the first genuine absinthe legally allowed to be imported into the United States since 1912. TTB approved the sale of Kübler Absinthe in the United States in May 2007. Thanks to the exhaustive work of both of the teams at Kübler and Viridian Spirits, absinthe can now be enjoyed in the United States.

THE LEGAL DETAILS

According to the Virtual Absinthe Museum, the legal requirements for absinthe to be sold in the United States state that any absinthe must be what the FDA considers "thujone-free," which means ten parts per million or less of thujone in the product. When it comes to labeling, the term *absinthe* may not be used as the brand name or fanciful name, and it must not simply stand alone on the product's label.

Images on the product's label must not allude to or show pictures that depict hallucinogenic, psychotropic, or mind-altering effects. In addition, according to the Code of Federal Regulations (21 CFR 172.510), domestic producers and importers of products using *Artemisia absinthium,* or other ingredients containing thujone, must submit a sample to the Beverage Alcohol Laboratory for thujone testing before seeking label approval.

EUROPE LIFTS ITS
ABSINTHE BAN

In 1988 absinthe was made legal in the European Community as long as the amount of thujone fell between ten parts per million and thirty-five parts per million. Meanwhile, in France, absinthe was allowed to be sold as long as it wasn't explicitly labeled as absinthe. Once again, everyone was getting caught up on the labels.

French absinthe makers worked around this regulation by simply labeling their product as *spiritueux à base de plantes d'absinthe,* or "wormwood-based spirits." However, to limit the production of absinthe products, government restrictions were also placed on fennel and hyssop, ingredients found in absinthe.

French distillers bypassed these restrictions by reducing the fennel and hyssop in their products or eliminating the herbs completely. These restrictions were repealed in 2009, and in April 2011 the French Senate voted for the re-legalization of absinthe for the first time in the country since 1915.

ABSINTHE IN MODERN-DAY NEW ORLEANS

Since the restrictions on absinthe have been lifted, New Orleans's connection to the liquor can again be felt throughout the city.

New Orleanian Jedd Haas was drawn to absinthe production because of its connection to New Orleans. He produces two kinds of absinthe at his distillery, Atelier Vie. Toulouse Green is traditional green absinthe that has a prominent wormwood flavor. Toulouse Red has an alluring reddish hue achieved with the addition of hibiscus. Its taste leans toward the sweeter side, thanks to the prominence of anise. Both of Haas's absinthes have a smooth finish and are meant to be enjoyed without the addition of sugar.

While researching this book, I was eager to learn about the history of absinthe, its relationship to New Orleans, and the Old Absinthe House. La Galerie de l'Absinthe at the Southern Food & Beverage Museum (SoFAB) in New Orleans was a great place to start.

La Galerie de l'Absinthe, New Orleans. Photograph by the author.

Absinthe historian Ray Bordelon and founder and curator of SoFAB, Elizabeth M. Williams, have amassed a beautiful collection of everything absinthe related at La Galerie de l'Absinthe. Here, at the only absinthe museum of its kind, you can explore an assortment of absinthe spoons, articles, historical replicas, and much more.

Green display cases are filled with vintage absinthe bottles and glasses, and one can't help but wonder about the stories that these old bottles hold. Bordelon's research into absinthe's history is extensive, right down to specific dates and shipping receipts. La Galerie de l'Absinthe should be added to any list of "can't miss" New Orleans spots, especially for anyone fascinated with this alluring spirit.

If you're looking to learn not just about absinthe but about American cocktails of all kinds, check out the Museum of the American Cocktail. Also located at the Southern Food & Beverage Museum, it's an excellent place for any cocktail lover who enjoys a little history with their favorite libation.

If you're interested in collecting some tools to begin your absinthe journey, some smaller shops might be a good place to start. For example, while hunting for a local place where I could find an absinthe fountain and absinthe spoons, I came across French Antique Shop, at 225 Royal Street in New Orleans. This shop sells reproductions of antique nineteenth-century absinthe fountains and an assortment of absinthe spoons and glasses for absinthe preparation. While the fountain may be out of the price range for a casual absinthe drinker, the spoons and glasses would be a beautiful addition to any absinthe lover's collection.

Maison Absinthe is an online shop where I have procured a few absinthe accessories. This store sells fountains, brouilleurs, spoons, glasses, carafes, and an array of other accoutrements that are perfect for any absinthe connoisseur or novice.

CHAPTER SIX

ABSINTHE COCKTAILS

AND WHERE TO FIND AN ABSINTHE FRAPPÉ IN NEW ORLEANS

RECIPES

Now that you know the history of absinthe, you might want to try your hand at mixing your own absinthe cocktails. Here are some delicious recipes that you can make at home. Remember that during the ban, Herbsaint was used in place of absinthe, so you may use either spirit in any of these recipes.

Check out the book *Famous New Orleans Drinks and How to Mix 'Em* by Stanley Clisby Arthur if you're thirsty for more. Initially published in 1937, it's full of cocktail recipes for drinks that you've heard of and many that you probably haven't. Another good cocktail book is *The Savoy Cocktail Book* by Harry Craddock. Initially published in 1930, it's a must for any cocktail lover's collection.

Star anise pods.

ABSINTHE FRAPPÉ

Cayetano's invention and the inspiration for this book! This drink is said to have helped put Old Absinthe House on the map. There are a few variations of this classic, so I've included an alternative recipe for the frappé by New Orleans bartender Chris Hannah. His version includes both absinthe and Herbsaint.

1½ ounces absinthe	2 ounces soda water
½ ounce simple syrup	Mint, for garnish

Add absinthe and simple syrup to a cocktail shaker and fill three-quarters with ice. Shake until chilled and strain into a double rocks glass with crushed ice. Add soda water and top with more crushed ice and garnish with a sprig of mint.

Chris Hannah's version:

1 ounce absinthe	2 ounces club soda
¾ ounce Herbsaint	Peychaud's bitters
¼ ounce Orgeat syrup	

Stir the ingredients until properly chilled and diluted. Add an ounce of club soda to an ice-filled collins glass and strain the cocktail over the ice and soda. Top with another ounce of club soda. Garnish with two or three dashes of Peychaud's bitters.

ABSINTHE PUNCH

This recipe, found in *Mixology: The Art of Preparing All Kinds of Drinks* by Joseph L. Haywood, published in 1898, was a popular party drink for its time. Absinthe Punch is meant to be enjoyed in a group.

1 glass absinthe
½ glass cognac
1 tablespoon sugar
1 tablespoon Orgeat syrup
Juice from one-half lemon

Combine all ingredients into a large bar glass with ice. Stir well and serve over ice with a straw.

ABSINTHE SUISSESSE

This classic New Orleans cocktail is a popular drink to enjoy at brunch. Recipes vary—this recipe is by bartender Chris Hannah.

1 ounce absinthe
½ ounce Herbsaint
½ ounce white crème de menthe
¼ ounce Orgeat syrup
1 fresh egg white
1 ounce half-and-half

Shake all ingredients without ice for about ten seconds, then add ice and shake until well chilled. Strain into a chilled wine glass.

BITTER PARTY OF ONE

Master mixologist Max Barwick won the grand prize at the 2018 Lucid Cocktail Classique with this cocktail inspired by spices that are usually found in a tiki drink. His goal was to pack flavor into the cocktail with as few ingredients as possible.

½ ounce Lucid Absinthe Supérieure
½ ounce Angostura bitters
½ ounce Angostura 1919 rum
¾ ounce lime juice
1 ounce Falernum

Combine all ingredients into a shaker; fill with ice and shake. Fine strain into a Nick and Nora glass. Garnish with fresh fennel greens laid on top of the glass like a crown or cap.

Recipe courtesy of Lucid Absinthe Supérieure.

COCKTAIL À LA LOUISIANE

This cocktail's history begins at the New Orleans restaurant La Louisiane. Opened in 1881 in the French Quarter, La Louisiane was founded by Antoine Alciatore, of Antoine's Restaurant fame. This drink is said to be a nod to the multicultural spirit of New Orleans.

¾ **ounce rye**

¾ **ounce Benedictine**

¾ **ounce sweet vermouth**

3 dashes Peychaud's bitters

3 dashes Herbsaint or absinthe

2 cherries for garnish

Combine all ingredients with ice and stir. Strain into a cocktail glass and garnish with cherries.

Recipe courtesy of Antoine's Restaurant.

CORPSE REVIVER NO. 2

This cocktail promised to "raise the dead" or cure a hangover. This is a classic brunch cocktail featured in Craddock's *The Savoy Cocktail Book.*

1 dash absinthe

¾ ounce dry gin

¾ ounce Lillet Blanc

¾ ounce orange liqueur

¾ ounce lemon juice

Rinse the inside of a cocktail glass with absinthe and discard the absinthe. Add gin, Lillet Blanc, orange liqueur, and lemon juice into a shaker with ice. Shake until well chilled and strain into the cocktail glass.

DEATH IN THE AFTERNOON

Invented by Ernest Hemingway, this cocktail is also known simply as the Hemingway or the Hemingway Champagne.

1½ ounces absinthe
4½ ounces chilled champagne or sparkling wine

Pour absinthe into a champagne flute, adding champagne or sparkling wine until a milky cloud appears.

MORNING CALL

When I found this cocktail in *The Complete Buffet Guide, or How to Mix All Kinds of Drinks* by V. B. Lewis, published in 1903, I was intrigued by its similarity to the Brunelle Cocktail, which was later published in *The Savoy Cocktail Book* by Harry Craddock. Morning Call uses Maraschino liqueur, whereas the Brunelle Cocktail uses sugar.

¼ ounce absinthe
½ ounce Maraschino liqueur
¾ ounce lemon or lime juice

Combine all ingredients, shake well, and pour into a bar glass with shaved ice. Serve with a straw.

THE NECROMANCER

Mayur Subbarao created this cocktail for Louro Restaurant in New York's West Village. This twist on the Corpse Reviver is meant to highlight the anise and fennel flavors in the drink as well as the cocktail's citrus and floral notes.

¾ ounce absinthe
¾ ounce elderflower liqueur
¾ ounce Lillet Blanc
1 dash London dry gin
¾ ounce lemon juice

Combine absinthe, elderflower liqueur, Lillet Blanc, dry gin, and lemon juice in a shaker with ice. Shake well until chilled. Strain into a coupe glass.

SAZERAC

The Sazerac was invented in the mid-nineteenth century in New Orleans and is not only one of the most famous absinthe cocktails but is also considered America's first cocktail. The Sazerac is the official cocktail of New Orleans, and the touch of absinthe gives a perfect hint of anise that balances out the drink's sweeter flavors.

1 cube sugar
3 dashes Peychaud's bitters
1½ ounces Sazerac Rye Whiskey
¼ ounce absinthe or Herbsaint

Pack an old-fashioned glass with ice. In a second old-fashioned glass, place the sugar cube, add Peychaud's bitters, and then crush the sugar cube. Add Sazerac Rye Whiskey to the second glass containing the Peychaud's bitters and sugar. Remove the ice from the first glass, coat the glass with absinthe, and discard the remaining absinthe. Empty the whiskey-bitters-sugar mixture from the second glass into the first glass and garnish with lemon peel.

Recipe courtesy of the Sazerac Company, www.sazerac.com.

TRINITY CHIMES

This is another interesting absinthe cocktail I found in Haywood's *Mixology: The Art of Preparing All Kinds of Drinks.* Trinity Chimes is a little sweet without being overpowering, and the absinthe adds a nice balance to the flavors.

1 ounce simple syrup

1 ounce vermouth

1 ounce orange bitters

1 ounce absinthe

1 ounce Benedictine

1 ounce gin

Cherry (optional)

Combine ingredients into a bar glass two-thirds filled with ice. Stir well and strain into a glass with a stem. Add cherry garnish, if desired.

WHERE TO FIND AN
ABSINTHE FRAPPÉ IN NEW ORLEANS

Whether you're looking for something with absinthe or another drink that will tickle your fancy, New Orleans is the best city in the world to enjoy a tasty cocktail. Here are some cocktail bars and restaurants you should visit whether you're a native New Orleanian or you're paying the city a visit. All of these bars serve the absinthe frappé and have a menu full of other delicious cocktails too.

ANTOINE'S RESTAURANT
713 St. Louis St. | 504.581.4422 | antoines.com

Considered one of the premiere restaurants in New Orleans, Antoine's has been serving fine food and drinks since 1840. Stop into the Hermes Bar at Antoine's and sample an absinthe frappé in an upscale casual atmosphere.

BAR TONIQUE
820 N. Rampart St. | 504.324.6045 | bartonique.com

Opened in 2008, Bar Tonique prides itself on being the first free-standing cocktail bar in New Orleans. Here you can enjoy finely crafted cocktails, wine, and beer in an unpretentious atmosphere.

CURE

4905 Freret St. | 504.302.2537 | curenola.com

Since 2009 Cure has served the Freret neighborhood with delicious, finely crafted cocktails in a friendly atmosphere. Cure has racked up such honors as being named one of "America's Best Bars" by *Esquire* and one of the "Best Cocktail Bars in the US" by *Food & Wine,* and it received an award for its "Outstanding Bar Program" from the James Beard Foundation in 2018.

FRENCH 75 BAR

813 Bienville St. | 504.523.5433 | arnaudsrestaurant.com

Inspired by France, French 75 Bar is considered an authentic New Orleans cocktail bar. The bar's high-quality cocktails are handcrafted by some of the best bartenders in the city, using locally sourced ingredients and liqueurs.

JEWEL OF THE SOUTH

1026 St. Louis St. | 504.265.8816 | jewelnola.com

Since 2019, owners Nick Detrich and Chris Hannah have offered handcrafted cocktails at Jewel of the South, which shares a name with a mid-nineteenth-century bar owned by Joseph Santini.

MR. B'S BISTRO

201 Royal St. | 504.523.2078 | mrbsbistro.com

Founded by Cindy Brennan, Mr. B's Bistro has become synonymous with upscale casual dining and delicious Cajun food. The absinthe frappé here is made with egg white and is served in a martini glass with no ice and has a bit of a mint flavor.

OLD ABSINTHE HOUSE

240 Bourbon St. | 504.523.3181

ruebourbon.com/old-absinthe-house

The Old Absinthe House has a long history and, in its early days, was the place to be if you wanted any cocktail made with absinthe. This is where the absinthe frappé was invented, but these days the bar's specialty is the Herbsaint frappé. Of course, you can order an absinthe frappé if you desire.

PIRATE'S ALLEY CAFÉ

622 Pirates Alley | 504.524.9332 | piratesalleycafe.com

Located in Pirates Alley, steps away from St. Louis Cathedral and the Cabildo, Pirate's Alley Café is known for its absinthe. Here you will enjoy an absinthe frappé served traditionally in the bar's lovely courtyard.

PEYCHAUD'S

727 Toulouse St. | 504.324.4888

maisondeville.com/peychaud-s

Owned by the same team as Cure, Peychaud's brings that old-time feel to the New Orleans cocktail bar scene. There's an extensive cocktail menu here that honors New Orleans's classic drinks.

Old Absinthe House sign, New Orleans. Courtesy photographer
David Rodrigue.

REVEL CAFÉ & BAR

133 N. Carrollton Ave. | 504.309.6122 | revelcafeandbar.com

Owner Chris McMillian is a fourth-generation bartender as well as a cocktail historian. He is a cofounder of the Museum of the American Cocktail. What better place to enjoy a cocktail and maybe hear a good story? Revel Café & Bar is a must-visit for any fine cocktail enthusiast.

THE COLUMNS

3811 St. Charles Ave. | 504.899.9308 | thecolumns.com

Set in an 1883 Italianate mansion under the oaks of St. Charles Avenue, the Columns hotel is the picture of elegance. Enjoy a cocktail at the ornate bar here or on the hotel's beautiful porch or patio. The bartenders here are experts, and their cocktails are crafted to perfection.

SOURCES

"Absinthe Frappe." Sheet Music Singer. https://www.sheetmusicsinger .com/absinthe-frappe.

"Absinthe Made His Heart Grow Fonder." *Washington Post,* December 10, 2007. http://voices.washingtonpost.com/small-business/2007/12 /absinthe_made_his_heart_grow_f.html.

Arthur, Stanley Clisby. *Famous New Orleans Drinks, and How to Mix 'Em.* New Orleans: Harmanson Publications, 1938.

Baker, Phil. *The Book of Absinthe: A Cultural History.* New York: Grove Press, 2001.

Baudelaire, Charles. *Les Fleurs du mal / The Flowers of Evil.* 1857 ed. Fleursdumal .org. https://fleursdumal.org/1857-table-of-contents.

———. *Les Paradis artificiels: Opium et haschisch.* Paris: Poulet-Malassis et de broise, 1860.

Bellucci, Laura. *The Belle Époque Guide to Absinthe.* New Orleans, 2019. https://static1.squarespace.com/static/5d0a68cffcce7c0001c84b00/t /5d532ae4a200020001a59e05/1565731566520/belleepoque-guideto absinthe-print.pdf.

"Best Cocktail Bars in the U.S." *Food & Wine,* March 26, 2019. https://www .foodandwine.com/travel/best-cocktail-bars-us.

Bordelon, Ray. Interview with author interview, October 10, 2021.

Breaux, Theodore. Interview and email exchange with author, October 24 and November 18 and 22, 2021.

Brister, Nancy. "The Old Absinthe House." Old New Orleans. www.old-new -orleans.com/NO_Absinthe_House.html.

Conrad, Barnaby, III. *Absinthe: History in a Bottle.* San Francisco: Chronicle Books, 1988.

Craddock, Harry. *The Savoy Cocktail Book.* London: Constable & Co., 1930.

Crowley, Aleister. "Absinthe: The Green Goddess." *The International* 12, no. 2 (February 1918). Musée Virtuel de l'Absinthe. www.museeabsinthe .com/Crowley-Green-Goddess.pdf.

"Distillerie Henri-Louis-Pernod (Caves Byrrh)." *Difford's Guide.* https:// www.diffordsguide.com/producers/291/distillerie-henri-louis-pernod -caves-byrrh.

"Edgar Allan Poe, Drugs, and Alcohol." The Edgar Allan Poe Society of Baltimore. https://www.eapoe.org/geninfo/poealchl.htm.

Haas, Jedd. Interview with author, October 9, 2021.

Haywood, Joseph L. *Mixology: The Art of Preparing All Kinds of Drinks.* Wilmington, DE: Press of the Sunday Star, 1898.

Hémard, Ned. "Absinthe and Athletics." New Orleans Nostalgia: Remembering New Orleans History, Culture and Traditions. New Orleans Bar Association. Amazon Web Services.

———. "Absinthe Minded." New Orleans Nostalgia: Remembering New Orleans History, Culture and Traditions. New Orleans Bar Association. Amazon Web Services.

Hicks, Jesse. "The Devil in a Little Green Bottle: A History of Absinthe." Distillations, Science History Institute. www.sciencehistory.org/distilla tions/the-devil-in-a-little-green-bottle-a-history-of-absinthe.

Joachim, H. *The Papyrus Ebers.* Translated by Cyril P. Bryan. London: G. Bles, 1930.

Lanier, Doris. *Absinthe, The Cocaine of the Nineteenth Century: A History of the Hallucinogenic Drug and Its Effect on Artists and Writers in Europe and the United States.* Jefferson: McFarland & Co., 1995.

Lehrman, Robert C. "Absinthe in America—US Legalization in 2007." Virtual Absinthe Museum. www.bevlaw.com/absintheinamerica.

Lewis, V. B. *The Complete Buffet Guide, or How to Mix All Kinds of Drinks.* Chicago: M. A. Donohue & Co., 1903.

Naifeh, Steven, and Gregory White Smith. *Van Gogh: The Life.* New York: Random House Trade Paperbacks, 2012.

Tuxedo No. 2. Website. https://tuxedono2.com/recipes.

Underwood, Vernon Philip. "Paul Verlaine." *Encyclopedia Britannica,* March 26, 2022. www.britannica.com/biography/Verlaine-Paul.

Verlaine, Paul. *Confessions.* Paris, 1895.

"Vincent Van Gogh: The Letters." Van Gogh Museum. Last updated October 2021, http://vangoghletters.org/vg/by_correspondent.html?correspondent=Theo_van_Gogh.

White, Edmund. *Rimbaud: The Double Life of a Rebel.* London: Atlas, 2008.

Williams, Elizabeth M. Interview with author, October 28, 2021.

Wondrich, David. "The Best Bars in America: 2011." *Esquire,* May 23, 2011. https://www.esquire.com/food-drink/bars/reviews/a9978/cure-bar-0611.

———. "The Fascinating History of New Orleans' Oldest Bar." Half Full. *Daily Beast,* January 26, 2019. Last updated February 6, 2019, www.thedailybeast.com/the-fascinating-history-of-new-orleans-oldest-bar.

WEBSITES OF INTEREST

Alandia Absinthe, alandia.de

Author's website, mariellesongy.com

Atelier Vie Distillery, ateliervie.com

David Rodrigue, djrstudios.com

Jade Liqueurs Fine Absinthes, jadeliqueurs.com

Lucid Absinthe Supérieure, drinklucid.com

Maison Absinthe, maisonabsinthe.com

Southern Food & Beverage Museum, southernfood.org

Wormwood Society, wormwoodsociety.org

ICONIC NEW ORLEANS COCKTAILS

The Sazerac

The Café Brûlot

The Vieux Carré

The Absinthe Frappé